Tom's Cake

"What can I do now?"

"I'm hungry!"

"No!"

"Cake? Yes!"

2

"I can make a cake."

3

"Butter"

"Milk"

"An egg"

"Flour"

4

"Chocolate. Good!"

"Banana and coffee"

5

"Now what?"

"Mix it up!"

"Wow!"

"Hi Mom!"

"Look at this."

Kate's Lunch

**"It's Saturday.
It's my birthday!"**

"Come to lunch. Bring food."

"Please come at
12 o'clock."

"Hi!"
"Happy Birthday, Kate!"

"Thanks!"

"Here you are."

"Thank you."

"What's this?"

"...and what's this?"

"Ice cream?"
"Chocolate! Yes, please."

Activities

Before you read

1. Look in the book.
    Is it  happy or 😊 sad?

After you read

2. Color
    1 = white
    2 = brown
    3 = blue
    4 = red

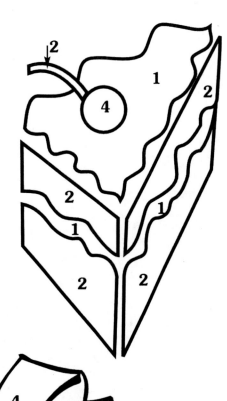

15

Pearson Education Limited
Edinburgh Gate, Harlow
Essex CM20 2JE, England
and Associated Companies throughout the world.

ISBN 0582 34414X

First published 2000

3 5 7 9 10 8 6 4

Text copyright © Audrey McIlvain 2000
Text photographs copyright © Frank Hopkinson 2000 '
Series Editors: Annie Hughes and Melanie Williams

Design by Neil Alexander

Printed in Scotland by Scotprint, Haddington

Published by Pearson Education Limited in association with Penguin Books Ltd,
both companies being subsidiaries of Pearson Plc

For a complete list of the titles available in the Penguin Young Readers series please write to your
local Pearson Education office or to: Penguin Readers Marketing Department, Pearson Education,
Edinburgh Gate, Harlow, Essex CM20 2JE